For information contact:
c/o Warrior Made
PO Box 1420, Santa Cruz, CA 95060
WarriorMade.com

Book and Cover Design by Andrea Horowitt
Production Director Ben Chargin
Recipe Cover Photos by Elisa Silva
Introduction Edited by Mara Waldhorn
Editing Contributors Bianca Silva and Shelby Clemons

Property of Warrior Made ISBN 9780997770377
First Edition March 2019
10 9 8 7 6 5 4 3 2 1

The KETO CARBS Cookbook

WITH ELISA SILVA

CONTENTS

INTRODUCTION	8
TWO-INGREDIENT KETO PASTA	12
GARLIC ORECCHEITTE	16
BISCUITS	19
THREE-SEED DINNER ROLLS	21
THREE-CHEESE RAVIOLI	24
CAULIFLOWER TORTILLAS	26
FATHEAD GNOCCHI	28
GARLIC KNOTS	30
GARLIC NAAN	33
HAMBURGER BUNS	35
ITALIAN BREAD STICKS	36
BLENDER EGG NOODLES	37
PUMPKIN GNOCCHI	39
LOW-CARB WRAPS	41
OLIVE FOCACCIA BREAD	43
OOPSIE FLAT BREAD	45
FATHEAD LASAGNA NOODLES	47
PITA BREAD	49
PRIMAL SOUL BREAD	50
ZESTY LEMON PASTA	51
FARFALLE	54
PULL-APART DINNER ROLLS	57
SIMPLE WHITE BREAD	60
SPINACH RICOTTA RAVIOLI	62
SOFT PRETZELS	65
SOURDOUGH BAGUETTES	67
SPINACH FETA BREAD	68
HERBED LINGUINE	69
FETTUCCINE	71
ALMOND FLOUR FETTUCCINE	72
CHEESY GARLIC BREAD	73
CAULIFLOWER BREAD BUNS	74
CHEESY ROSEMARY	75
FOCACCIA BREAD	75
ITALIAN CLOUD BREAD	77
CROISSANTS	80
COCONUT FLOUR BREAD	82
ENGLISH MUFFINS	83
EVERYTHING BAGELS	85
FATHEAD PIZZA CRUST	87
FLAX TORTILLAS	88
FRENCH BRIOCHE	89
HERBED CAVATELLI	90
PAN FRIED GNOCCHI	92
FATHEAD BUNS	93

INTRODUCTION

Everybody loves bread, but anyone who's doing the keto diet knows carbs are bad. Carbohydrates are one of the things you miss the most doing keto. What if I told you that you could still have bread and even pasta? In this cookbook, you will find 47 keto-friendly breads and pastas that won't knock you off track!

Now, the reason why I created a keto-friendly recipe book in the first place is that I know how big of a struggle weight loss can be, especially if you are new to the keto diet. On the one hand, you want to reach your goal weight, and you want to make sure you aren't taking in too many high-carb foods. On the other hand, I know you want to enjoy what you're eating.

You don't want to feel like you're suffering all the way through every meal.

Let me tell you a little bit about the keto diet, so you can see why the recipes I'm about to give you are so amazing.

WHAT IS KETO?

The keto diet is a low-carb, high-fat diet. Normally, your body takes the carbs you eat and turns them into glucose. Glucose is a simple sugar, and your cells need glucose for energy. Any time there isn't enough glucose in your bloodstream for energy, your body turns on a "switch," if you will, and burns fat for energy instead. Whenever your body is burning fat instead of glucose, it's in a state called ketosis. Ketosis is the reason why the keto diet is all the rage — by eliminating carbs and sugar, your body burns fat. Now, keto isn't a fix-all diet — it takes consistency to see results. But, once you start seeing the benefits, they truly are amazing. The goal of this cookbook is to help you make sure you do two things well.

KETO GOAL #1: NEVER GO OVER 5 TO 10% CARBS IN YOUR DIET IN A SINGLE DAY

The keto concept itself is simple. It consists of no sugar, low carbs, and high fats and proteins. However, the way that looks is different for everyone. People who begin the keto diet typically starts by dropping their carb intake to around 50 net carbs a day. From there, it is up to you to find the perfect balance for your body.

KETO GOAL #2: NEVER CREATE DISGUSTING MEALS JUST BECAUSE YOU'RE ON A DIET

These recipes are hand-selected and tested, so you know that they are amazing, and you'll never feel like you're trading enjoyment for your goal of looking your best.

HOW TO GET MAXIMUM RESULTS USING THIS COOKBOOK

Now, although keto is mainly comprised of carb restrictions and no sugars, the best results are achieved when you combine this way of eating with a cheat day and intermittent fasting.

I have always lived by the philosophy that humans were intended to eat a simple diet comprised of real foods.

Early humans were hunters and gatherers, and our bodies still crave things that are healthy. We still need whole food. With these recipes, you'll be able to stay away from the processed ingredients that are so popular right now. Doing keto doesn't mean you have to avoid having bread or pasta now and then. But, you also don't want to knock yourself out of ketosis by putting too many carbs in your diet.

Here at Warrior Made, our goal is to meet you wherever you are and provide you with recipes that will make your life simpler and healthier. The keto diet is a tool for your journey. This book is here to help you achieve balance and succeed on your keto journey. We recommend using the concepts seen in this "Keto Carbs" cookbook.

Elisa Silva

Chef Elisa
For more information, visit WarriorMade.com

TWO-INGREDIENT KETO PASTA

PREP TIME 10 MINUTES | COOK TIME 1 MINUTE | SERVES 1

1 cup mozzarella cheese, shredded

1 large egg

Pinch of salt

Calories per serving 408
Total fat 30g
Total carbohydrates 3g
Fiber 0g; *Net carbs 3g*
Protein 31g

Directions

For the dough:

In a saucepan, melt the mozzarella over low heat, stirring continuously so it doesn't burn. Stir until cheese is completely melted.

Remove from heat and allow the mozzarella to cool for 1 minute, so that it will not cook the egg.

Lightly beat the egg, next add to the cheese, and mix until you have a uniform yellow dough.

Place the dough on a flat surface lined with parchment paper with another piece of parchment paper on top of the dough.

With a rolling pin, roll dough until it is ⅛-inch thick.

Remove the top piece of parchment and slice the dough into ½-inch wide strips. Refrigerate the dough for at least 6 hours or overnight.

Cooking the pasta:

Bring a pot of water to boil (do not add salt to the water). Add the prepped dough and cook for about 40 seconds to 1 minute (be careful not to cook too long or the pasta will lose its form).

Remove pasta from pot and run under cold water to cool it down. Carefully separate any strands sticking together. Allow pasta to cool until it is only slightly warm to the touch.

Serve with your favorite pasta sauce and season with salt.

GARLIC ORECCHEITTE

PREP TIME 40 MINUTES | COOK TIME 5 MINUTES | SERVES 4

For the pasta:

¾ cup almond flour

2 tablespoons coconut flour

2 teaspoons arrowroot powder

½ teaspoon garlic powder

¼ teaspoon kosher salt

2 teaspoons apple cider vinegar

1 egg lightly beaten

2-4 teaspoons water, as needed

Directions

In a food processor, combine almond flour, coconut flour, arrowroot powder, garlic powder, and salt. Pulse until well combined.

With the food processor running, add in apple cider vinegar. Once it has distributed evenly, add in the egg.

Add water teaspoon by teaspoon, as needed — while the food processor is still running — until the dough forms into a ball. The dough should be firm, but sticky to touch and with no creases.

Remove dough from the food processor. Wrap dough in plastic wrap and knead it through the plastic for a couple of minutes.

Place the dough in the refrigerator to rest for 30 minutes (or up to 5 days).

To shape, cut the dough into 4 pieces. Roll out each of the 4 pieces into logs, and slice off even-sized pieces. Using your thumb, press each piece against your opposite palm, creating an indentation. Lightly dust with coconut flour as needed. You can either leave them as they are or turn them out.

In a skillet over low heat, add butter and oil. Once warm, add in chilled pasta and toss.

Cook pasta until it just begins to develop some color (this will give the most *al dente* texture).

Serve with freshly grated Parmesan or your favorite toppings.

For cooking:

3 tablespoons grass-fed butter

2 tablespoons avocado oil

Calories per serving 207
Total fat 20g
Total carbohydrates 5g
Fiber 2g; *Net carbs 3g*
Protein 3g

BISCUITS

PREP TIME 10 MINUTES | COOK TIME 10 MINUTES | MAKES 9 BISCUITS

1 ½ cups superfine almond flour

¼ teaspoon salt

1 tablespoon baking powder

½ teaspoon garlic powder

2 large eggs

½ cup sour cream

4 tablespoons unsalted butter, melted

½ cup cheddar cheese, shredded

Calories per serving 232
Total fat 21g
Total carbohydrates 4g
Fiber 2g; *Net carbs 2g*
Protein 8g

Directions

Preheat oven to 450°F. Lightly grease a muffin pan.

In a large bowl, combine almond flour, salt, baking powder, and garlic powder.

In a small bowl, combine eggs, sour cream, and butter. Whisk until smooth, then add to the dry ingredients.

Add cheese and mix batter until all ingredients are thoroughly incorporated (batter will be quite thick).

Scoop ¼ cup of batter and drop into muffin mold and repeat until all the batter is used.

Bake the biscuits for about 10 to 11 minutes or until tops are golden and a toothpick comes out clean.

Allow the biscuits to cool slightly before serving.

THREE-SEED DINNER ROLLS

PREP TIME 10 MINUTES | COOK TIME 40 MINUTES | MAKES 6 ROLLS

1 ¼ cup almond flour

¼ cup coconut flour

¼ cup + 3 tablespoons ground psyllium husk

½ teaspoon salt

2 teaspoons baking powder

2 teaspoons apple cider vinegar

1 tablespoon avocado oil

2 ½ cups hot water

1 tablespoon sesame seeds

½ tablespoon poppy seeds

1 tablespoon sunflower seeds

Calories per serving 107
Total fat 8g
Total carbohydrates 5g
Fiber 102g; *Net carbs 7g*
Protein 4g

Directions

Preheat oven to 375°F and line a baking sheet with parchment paper.

In a large mixing bowl, combine all the dry ingredients — except the sesame, poppy, and sunflower seeds.

Add the apple cider vinegar, avocado oil, and slowly stir in the hot water. With a spatula, stir about 1 minute or until the water has absorbed (dough should be soft and sticky, but you should be able to form a ball with your hand. If not, add more psyllium husk 1 teaspoon at a time).

Set aside and allow to rest for 10 minutes.

Divide the dough into 6 small balls.

Roll each ball between your hands, and place them one by one on the baking tray.

With a pastry brush, lightly brush, the top of each bread ball with avocado oil.

Sprinkle the tops with the sesame, poppy, and sunflower seeds and bake for 40 to 45 minutes.

Remove from the oven and allow to cool completely on a cooling rack.

THREE CHEESE RAVIOLI

PREP TIME 45 MINUTES | COOK TIME 10 MINUTES | MAKES 20 RAVIOLI

For the dough:

1 cup almond flour

3 tablespoons coconut flour

2 teaspoons arrowroot powder

¼ teaspoon sea salt

2 teaspoons apple cider vinegar

1 egg, lightly beaten

3-5 teaspoons water

Directions

For the dough:

In a food processor, combine almond flour, coconut flour, and arrowroot powder. Pulse until thoroughly combined.

With the food processor running, pour in apple cider vinegar. Once it has distributed evenly, add the egg.

Teaspoon by teaspoon, slowly add in water until the dough forms into a ball (the dough should be firm, yet sticky to touch and with no creases, which means the dough is dry and you need to add a little more water).

Wrap dough in plastic wrap and knead it through the plastic for a couple of minutes.

Allow the dough to rest for 15 minutes at room temperature, then transfer to the fridge for 45 minutes.

For the filling:

In a large bowl, combine ricotta, mozzarella, and Parmesan cheese. Mix in egg yolks, and continue mixing until thoroughly combined. Season with salt and freshly ground pepper to taste and set aside.

For the ravioli.

Place the dough between two pieces of parchment paper and roll out the pasta to its thinnest point possible. Slice into 2-inch strips, and then cut into evenly sized squares about 2x2-inches.

Heap roughly a tablespoon of filling onto the dough. Drape a second piece over it, and press down around the edges to seal, removing any air bubbles.

Trim the edges close to the filling using a cookie cutter, knife, or pizza cutter.

Place all the ravioli on a baking tray and freeze for 15 minutes to firm them up.

To cook:

In a large skillet, add 1 tablespoon of olive oil and heat on low.

Add ravioli and cook until golden on both sides.

Toss with your favorite sauce to serve.

For the filling:

1 cup ricotta cheese

1 cup mozzarella cheese, grated

⅔ cup Parmesan cheese, freshly grated

Salt and ground black pepper, to taste

2 egg yolks

Olive oil, for cooking

Calories per serving 120
Total fat 6g
Total carbohydrates 13g
Fiber 5g; *Net carbs 8g*
Protein 4g

CAULIFLOWER TORTILLAS

PREP TIME 30 MINUTES | COOK TIME 20 MINUTES | MAKES 6 TORTILLAS

2 cups cauliflower

2 large eggs

¼ cup fresh cilantro, chopped

½ medium lime, juiced and zested

½ teaspoon garlic powder

Salt and ground black pepper, to taste

Calories per serving 36
Total fat 2g
Total carbohydrates 3g
Fiber 1g; *Net carbs 2g*
Protein 3g

Directions

Preheat the oven to 375°F. Line a baking sheet with parchment paper.

Cut cauliflower into small, uniform pieces, and pulse in a food processor in batches until you get a rice-like consistency.

Place the cauliflower in a steamer and cook until slightly tender.

Place the cauliflower a fine cheesecloth or thin dish towel. Squeeze out as much liquid as possible, being careful not to burn yourself.

In a medium bowl, whisk the eggs until frothy. Add in cauliflower, cilantro, lime, garlic powder, salt, and pepper. Mix until thoroughly combined.

Use your hands to form 6 small "tortillas" on parchment paper.

Bake for 10 minutes and carefully flip each tortilla. Return to the oven and bake for an additional 5 to 7 minutes, or until completely set.

Place tortillas on a wire rack to cool slightly.

Heat a medium-sized skillet over medium heat. Place a baked tortilla in the pan, press down slightly with a spatula, and brown for 1 to 2 minutes on each side.

Repeat with remaining tortillas.

FATHEAD GNOCCHI

PREP TIME 10 MINUTES | SERVES 4

2 cups superfine blanched almond flour

2 cups full-fat mozzarella cheese, shredded

¼ cup butter

1 large egg

1 large egg yolk

¼ teaspoon salt

¼ teaspoon garlic powder

Calories per serving 634
Total fat 54g
Total carbohydrates 8g
Fiber 6g; *Net carbs 2g*
Protein 30g

Directions

In a saucepan over low heat combine butter and mozzarella. Stir continuously until completely melted.

Stir vigorously with a rubber spatula until fully combined, and then cool for 2 minutes.

In a large bowl combine egg, egg yolk and almond flour.

Slowly add the cheese mixture and continue to mix until a rough dough is formed.

Transfer the dough onto a smooth surface (or parchment paper) and knead until a semi-stretchy dough is formed. (if the dough is too wet, add a tablespoon or more of almond flour)

Form the dough into a long roll about 1 inch thick and begin to cut pieces about ½-inch wide.

Freeze the gnocchi for 15 minutes before cooking, or freeze them until ready to eat.

Bring a pot of salted water to a gentle boil (if it's too vigorous and the gnocchi will fall apart).

Add gnocchi to the water in small batches and boil for 1 to 2 minutes, or until they float to the surface.

Remove gnocchi with a slotted spoon and place on a paper towel. Allow to cool for 5 minutes.

Gently toss gnocchi with your favorite sauce and serve!

GARLIC KNOTS

For the dough:

6 ounces mozzarella cheese, shredded

3 ounces superfine almond flour

4 tablespoons cream cheese

1 large egg

2 teaspoons dried basil

1 teaspoon garlic powder

1 teaspoon baking powder

½ teaspoon salt

Avocado oil (for top of knots)

Directions

Preheat the oven to 375°F. Line a baking sheet with parchment paper.

In a large bowl, combine all dry ingredients and mix thoroughly.

In a saucepan over low heat, add mozzarella cheese and cream cheese. Stir until the cheese is completely melted.

Add the melted cheese mixture to the dry ingredients, and stir until a dough begins to form

Add the egg, stirring it in until absorbed and well mixed. Allow the dough to cool enough to be handled.

Remove from the bowl and cut the dough into 8 equal pieces.

Roll each piece into a log about 9-inches long, and form into a knot-like shape.

Place the knots at least 1 inch apart on the prepared, lined baking sheet. Lightly brush the tops with avocado oil.

Bake for about 15 minutes or until the tops are lightly golden. Remove from the oven, and set the broiler on high.

In a small saucepan over low heat, combine butter and minced garlic. Heat until butter is melted and garlic is fragrant.

Brush the garlic butter over the tops of the knots and sprinkle Parmesan cheese on top.

Return the garlic knots to the oven and broil until golden brown on top, about 1 minute.

For the toppings:

3 cloves garlic, minced

1 tablespoon butter

1 tablespoon Parmesan cheese, finely grated

Calories per serving 189
Total fat 16g
Total carbohydrates 3g
Fiber 2g; *Net carbs 1g*
Protein 9g

GARLIC NAAN

½ cup coconut flour

1 ½ tablespoons psyllium husk powder

2 tablespoons avocado oil

¼ teaspoon baking powder

1-1 ½ cups hot water

1 tablespoon garlic, minced

¼ teaspoon salt

Calories per serving 343
Total fat 23g
Total carbohydrates 14g
Fiber 22g; *Net carbs 8g*
Protein 10g

Directions

Combine the coconut flour, psyllium husk powder, baking powder, minced garlic, salt, and avocado oil.

Slowly add 1 cup of hot water (if necessary, add more hot water).

Knead with your hands until all of the ingredients are well incorporated.

Allow the dough to rest for 15 minutes.

Pull apart the dough into equally sized portions (you can make these as big or small as you like).

Place each ball in between two pieces of parchment paper, and roll out into a circle about ⅓-inch thick. Sprinkle with minced garlic, and press lightly into the dough.

Heat a lightly greased skillet to medium heat. Add a naan to the heated skillet, flipping after a couple minutes. Cook until browned on both sides, and the naan begins to puff up.

Repeat this process until all naans are cooked.

HAMBURGER BUNS

PREP TIME 5 MINUTES | COOK TIME 15 MINUTES | MAKES 5 BUNS

1 cup cheddar cheese, shredded

6 tablespoons almond flour

1 tablespoon Parmesan cheese

¼ teaspoon arrowroot powder

3 eggs

Calories per serving 151
Total fat 12g
Total carbohydrates 1g
Fiber 0g; *Net carbs 1g*
Protein 10g

Directions

Preheat oven to 350°F, and line a baking sheet with parchment paper.

In a large bowl, whisk eggs together.

Add remaining ingredients to the bowl and mix until thoroughly combined.

Scoop five spoonfuls of the mixture onto the baking sheet lined with parchment paper, and smooth the mixture into desired shape.

Bake for 10 to 12 minutes and then broil on high for 3 minutes.

Remove from oven, and allow to cool completely before using.

ITALIAN BREAD STICKS

PREP TIME 15 MINUTES | COOK TIME 20 MINUTES | SERVES 16

1 ½ cups almond flour

2 ½ cups mozzarella cheese, shredded

3 ounces cream cheese

2 eggs

2 tablespoons Parmesan cheese, grated

2 cloves garlic, finely minced

1 tablespoon psyllium husk powder

2 teaspoons baking powder

1 teaspoon garlic powder

2 teaspoons dried parsley

½ teaspoon dried basil

½ teaspoon dried oregano

Salt, to taste

Olive oil, for handling and forming the dough

Calories per serving 212
Total fat 25g
Total carbohydrates 5g
Fiber 3g; *Net carbs 2g*
Protein 17g

Directions

Preheat oven to 400˚F. Line a baking sheet with parchment paper.

In a saucepan over low heat, combine the shredded mozzarella and cream cheese. Stir continuously until completely melted.

In a separate bowl, combine the almond flour, psyllium husk powder, basil, oregano, parsley, salt, and baking powder.

Slowly add the eggs to the dry ingredients and begin mixing.

Add the cheese mixture and Parmesan, and mix until thoroughly combined (dough should be sticky to the touch).

Oil your hands to begin forming the bread sticks. Divide the dough into 8 pieces, then form into logs, and divide again into 16 bread sticks total.

Place on the baking sheet evenly spaced apart. Bake for 12 minutes rotating the pan halfway through.

Remove the bread sticks from the oven, and lightly brush olive oil over the tops. Bake for an additional 3 minutes.

Allow to cool slightly before serving.

BLENDER EGG NOODLES

1 ounce cream cheese, softened

2 eggs, room temperature

¼ teaspoon arrowroot powder

Pinch of salt

Calories per serving 125
Total fat 10g
Total carbohydrates 2g
Fiber 0g; *Net carbs 2g*
Protein 7g

Directions

Preheat the oven to 325°F. Line a baking sheet with parchment paper.

In a blender, combine all of the ingredients. Blend on high for 1 minute or until smooth. Pour onto prepared baking sheet.

Smooth out into a rectangle, keeping the batter very thin.

Bake for 5 minutes or until set. Be careful NOT to over-bake.

Remove from oven and allow to sit for a couple of minutes before cutting.

Slice into ¼-inch strips and toss with your favorite sauce.

PUMPKIN GNOCCHI

1 cup mozzarella cheese, shredded

1 cup Parmesan cheese, shredded

½ cup pumpkin puree

2 egg yolks

¼ teaspoon ground nutmeg

Almond flour, for coating gnocchi

Coconut oil, for frying

Calories per serving 317
Total fat 27g
Total carbohydrates 6g
Fiber 4g; *Net carbs 2g*
Protein 17g

Directions

In a saucepan over low heat, combine the Parmesan, pumpkin, ground nutmeg, and mozzarella. Stir continuously until completely melted.

Transfer cheese mixture to a large mixing bowl.

Add the egg yolks and knead with your hands until a dough begins to form.

Shape the dough into 3 long rolls about 2 inches in diameter, and wrap in plastic wrap.

Chill until firm or up to 3 days.

When ready to cook, remove the plastic wrap, and slice the gnocchi into ½-inch thick pieces.

Toss in almond flour until completely coated.

Heat a few tablespoons of oil in a large skillet until very hot.

Add a couple of the gnocchi at a time, shaking the pan to prevent them from sticking.

Cook for about 30 seconds on each side and remove from pan.

Once you have cooked all of the gnocchi, allow to sit for a couple minutes to firm up.

Toss gnocchi with your favorite sauce.

LOW-CARB WRAPS

PREP TIME 8 MINUTES | COOK TIME 20 MINUTES | SERVES 12

4 ounces plain pork rinds, crushed

⅛ teaspoon baking soda

¼ teaspoon salt

4 ounces cream cheese, softened

6 large eggs (cold)

½ cup water

Calories per serving 147
Total fat 11g
Total carbohydrates 1g
Fiber 0g; *Net carbs 1g*
Protein 12g

Directions

Place the pork rinds in a food processor, and process until they become a fine powder.

Add the baking soda and salt.

Add the eggs and cream cheese, and process until smooth.

Add the water, and blend until all of the ingredients are thoroughly combined.

Pour into a bowl, and let sit for 5 to 10 minutes or until the batter thickens.

Preheat a large skillet over medium heat. When hot, lightly oil the pan.

Using a ¼-cup, pour the batter onto the skillet, and spread into a 5-inch circle using the back of a large spoon.

Cook like you would a pancake.

Keep in the refrigerator for up to one week, or freeze with a piece of parchment paper between each wrap.

OLIVE FOCACCIA BREAD

4 ounces cream cheese, softened

4 ounces salted butter, softened

4 eggs

1 ¾ cups almond flour

1 teaspoon baking powder

¼ teaspoon of arrowroot powder

16 Kalamata olives, pitted and sliced

Sea salt

Calories per serving 346
Total fat 33g
Total carbohydrates 4g
Fiber 3g; **Net carbs 1g**
Protein 9g

Directions

Preheat your oven to 375°F, and line an 8x12-inch baking dish with parchment paper.

Using an electric mixer, combine the cream cheese and butter until fluffy.

Add the eggs one at a time, and beat until well incorporated.

Add the almond flour, baking powder, and arrowroot powder. Mix well.

Scoop the mixture into the baking dish and smooth out.

Top with the olives and sea salt.

Bake for 18 to 25 minutes or until it springs back when touched.

OOPSIE FLAT BREAD

3 eggs, separated

¼ teaspoon cream of tartar

3 ounces cream cheese, softened

Preferred herbs and spices, to taste

2 ounces Parmesan, grated

Calories per serving 152
Total fat 13g
Total carbohydrates 2g
Fiber 0g; *Net carbs 2g*
Protein 8g

Directions

Preheat oven to 300°F. Line a baking sheet with parchment paper.

In two bowls, separate the eggs. Beat egg whites with cream of tartar until stiff peaks form.

In a separate bowl, mix together egg yolks, spices/herbs of choice, and cream cheese.

Gently fold the yolk mixture into the egg whites (be careful not to break down the whites).

With a large spoon, scoop the batter into a round pile (about 6 to 10 inches) on the baking sheet.

Bake for about 30 minutes or until slightly golden brown.

Remove from oven and allow to cool on a rack (flat bread will deflate slightly).

Store your Oopsie Flat Bread in a loosely lidded container or in the refrigerator until you are ready to use.

Lightly brush top of Oopsie bread with olive oil, and top with cheese and dark greens like spinach or arugula.

Broil in the oven until cheese is melted and flat bread is slightly browned.

FATHEAD LASAGNA NOODLES

PREP TIME 10 MINUTES | COOK TIME 12-14 MINUTES | SERVES 8

¾ cup almond flour

1 ¾ cups mozzarella cheese, shredded

2 tablespoons cream cheese

1 egg

Pinch of salt

Calories per serving 128
Total fat 10g
Total carbohydrates 2g
Fiber 0g; *Net carbs 2g*
Protein 8g

Directions

Preheat oven to 400°F. Line a baking sheet with parchment paper.

In a saucepan over low heat, melt the cream cheese and mozzarella.

Once melted, completely remove from heat.

Stir in the almond flour, and mix until thoroughly combined.

Add the egg and salt, and stir until a dough has formed.

Transfer dough onto a large work surface. Shape dough into a ball, and place between two pieces of parchment paper.

Use a rolling pin on top of parchment paper to roll dough in a rectangular shape. Remove the top parchment paper, and slide dough onto baking sheet.

Bake for 12 to 14 minutes or until slightly brown. Cut into long lasagna "noodles" and set aside, or store in the refrigerator until ready to use.

PITA BREAD

¼ cup almond flour, firmly packed

1 tablespoon coconut flour, firmly packed

⅛ teaspoon baking soda

1 teaspoon psyllium husk powder

¼ cup hot water

1 egg

1 tablespoon avocado oil

Pinch of salt

Calories per serving 695
Total fat 51g
Total carbohydrates 6g
Fiber 1g; *Net carbs 5g*
Protein 56g

Directions

Preheat oven to 350°F. Line a baking sheet with parchment.

In a small bowl, combine all of the dry ingredients.

In a separate bowl, combine the wet ingredients, and whisk until well combined.

Incorporate the dry ingredients with the wet ingredients, and mix until a thick batter forms.

Between two pieces of parchment, roll the dough into 8-inch balls, and place on a baking sheet.

Bake 17 to 19 minutes.

Remove from the oven, and allow to cool on a wire rack.

Cut each circle in half, and cut a slit to make a pocket.

Store cooled pitas in an airtight container for up to 5 days.

PRIMAL SOUL BREAD

PREP TIME 10 MINUTES | COOK TIME 1 HOUR 5 MINUTES | MAKES 1

1 ½ cups cream cheese, softened

¼ cup butter, melted

¼ cup avocado oil

¼ cup heavy whipping cream

4 large eggs

1 ⅔ cups unflavored whey protein isolate

2 teaspoons cream of tartar

1 teaspoon baking soda

1 teaspoon xanthan gum

½ teaspoon salt

Calories per serving 546
Total fat 36g
Total carbohydrates 4g
Fiber 1g; *Net carbs 3g*
Protein 54g

Directions

Preheat the oven to 325°F. Lightly grease an 8x4-inch loaf pan.

In a large bowl, beat together cream cheese and salt using a hand whisk.

Add melted butter, avocado oil, heavy whipping cream, and eggs. Beat until thoroughly combined.

Add the baking soda, cream of tartar, xanthan gum, and whey protein isolate. Mix until batter is smooth, and there are no visible lumps.

Pour the batter in a loaf pan, and bake for 50 minutes or until an inserted toothpick comes out clean.

Place on a cooling rack for 10 to 15 minutes.

Slice and serve.

ZESTY LEMON PASTA

PREP TIME 15 MINUTES | COOK TIME 6-8 MINUTES | SERVES 1

2 tablespoons coconut flour + some for dusting

½ teaspoon arrowroot powder

¼ teaspoon baking powder

1 large egg, room temperature

½ lemon, juiced and zested

2 tablespoons olive oil

Salt, to taste

Fresh basil, optional

Calories per serving 382
Total fat 34g
Total carbohydrates 11g
Fiber 5g; *Net carbs 6g*
Protein 8g

Directions

In a large bowl, combine the coconut flour, arrowroot powder, baking powder, and salt.

Add the lemon juice, zest, and egg. Beat together until it forms a wet dough.

Allow to rest for about 20 minutes.

Transfer the dough onto a large sheet of parchment paper dusted with coconut flour, and dust the dough with additional coconut flour.

Place another sheet of parchment on top, and roll the ball out flat.

Slice into thick noodles.

Carefully transfer the noodles into a heat-safe, small bowl.

Place the bowl in a pot of water with the water reaching only about halfway up the sides of the bowl.

Cover and bring to a boil. Steam the noodles for about 6 to 8 minutes until the egg is completely cooked.

Carefully remove from the pot.

Toss in olive oil and fresh basil.

FARFALLE

PREP TIME 40 MINUTES | COOK TIME 5 MINUTES | SERVES 4

¾ cup almond flour

2 tablespoons coconut flour

2 teaspoons arrowroot powder

¼ teaspoon kosher salt

2 teaspoons apple cider vinegar

1 egg, lightly beaten

2-4 teaspoons water, as needed

Avocado oil, for cooking

Calories per serving 131
Total fat 11g
Total carbohydrates 5g
Fiber 2g; *Net carbs 3g*
Protein 3g

Directions

In a food processor, combine almond flour, coconut flour, arrowroot powder, and salt. Pulse until well combined.

With the food processor running, add in apple cider vinegar. Once it has distributed evenly, add in the egg.

Add water teaspoon by teaspoon, as needed, until the dough forms into a ball. The dough should be firm, but sticky to touch and with no creases.

Wrap dough in plastic wrap, and knead it through the plastic for a couple of minutes.

Place the dough in the refrigerator to rest for 30 minutes (or up to 5 days).

Roll out the pasta to its thinnest point with a pasta machine or a rolling pin. Cut into roughly 2x1-inch rectangles.

Gently pinch the center of each rectangle to create a bow-like shape.

Place shaped pasta in the freezer for 15 minutes (or up to a couple months until ready to use).

In a skillet over low heat, add butter and avocado oil. Once warm, add in chilled pasta and toss.

Cook pasta until it just begins to develop some color (this will give the most *al dente* texture).

Serve right away with your choice of toppings.

PULL-APART DINNER ROLLS

PREP TIME 25 MINUTES | COOK TIME 20 MINUTES | MAKES 24 ROLLS

8 ounces cream cheese

3 cups mozzarella cheese, shredded

4 large eggs

4 tablespoons baking powder

1 ⅓ cups almond flour

½ teaspoon garlic powder

1 tablespoon salted butter

Calories per serving 263
Total fat 22g
Total carbohydrates 3g
Fiber 2g; *Net carbs 1g*
Protein 12g

Directions

Preheat the oven to 400°F.

In a small pot over low heat, melt the mozzarella and cream cheese together. Stir until smooth and creamy.

In a large bowl, add the melted cheeses, baking powder, almond flour, garlic powder, and eggs.

Mix until well combined, and let sit for 10 to 20 minutes.

Divide the dough into 24 balls, and chill in the refrigerator for 15 minutes.

Melt the butter over low heat in a 10-inch cast iron skillet.

Place the dough balls into the skillet, so they are touching on each side.

Bake for 20 to 25 minutes until fluffy and golden brown.

Let cool and serve.

SIMPLE WHITE BREAD

PREP TIME 10 MINUTES | COOK TIME 1 HOUR 10 MINUTES | SERVES 18

1 cup almond flour

¼ cup coconut flour

2 teaspoons baking powder

⅓ cup butter, melted

12 large egg whites, room temperature

1 ½ tablespoons Swerve (optional)

¼ teaspoon arrowroot powder

¼ teaspoon cream of tartar

¼ teaspoon salt

Calories per serving 63
Total fat 5g
Total carbohydrates 2g
Fiber 1g; *Net carbs 1g*
Protein 3g

Directions

Preheat the oven to 325°F. Line an 8 ½ x 4 ½-inch loaf pan with parchment paper (leave extra hanging over the sides for easy removal).

In a food processor, combine the almond flour, coconut flour, baking powder, Swerve, arrowroot powder, and salt. Pulse until combined.

Slowly add the melted butter. Pulse until crumbly, scraping down the sides as needed.

Using an electric mixer, beat the egg whites and cream of tartar until stiff peaks form.

Add half of the egg whites to the food processor. Pulse a few times until just combined (do not over-mix).

Carefully transfer the mixture from the food processor into the bowl with the remaining egg whites. Gently fold until combined (do not stir).

Pour the batter into the loaf pan and smooth the top.

Bake for about 40 minutes or until the top is golden brown.

Create a tent with aluminum foil, and bake for an additional 30 to 45 minutes until the top is firm and the internal temperature is 200°F.

Allow to cool completely before removing from the pan and slicing.

SPINACH RICOTTA RAVIOLI

PREP TIME 45 MINUTES | COOK TIME 10 MINUTES | MAKES 20 RAVIOLI

For the dough:

1 cup almond flour

3 tablespoons coconut flour

2 teaspoons arrowroot powder

¼ teaspoon sea salt

2 teaspoons apple cider vinegar

1 egg, lightly beaten

3-5 teaspoons water

Directions

For the dough:

In a food processor, combine almond flour, coconut flour, salt, and arrowroot powder. Pulse until thoroughly combined.

With the food processor running, pour in apple cider vinegar. Once it has distributed evenly, add the egg.

Teaspoon by teaspoon, slowly add in water until the dough forms into a ball (the dough should be firm, yet sticky to touch and with no creases, which means the dough is dry and you need to add a little more water).

Wrap dough in plastic wrap, and knead it through the plastic for a couple minutes.

Allow the dough to rest for 15 minutes at room temperature, then transfer to the fridge for 45 minutes.

For the filling:

In a skillet over medium heat, heat up avocado oil.

Add garlic and sauté until it becomes fragrant and starts to soften.

Add spinach and reduce the heat. Once wilted, remove from the pan and squeeze out excess liquid, transfer it to a board, and roughly chop. Allow to cool.

In a medium bowl, combine spinach, ricotta, grated Parmesan cheese, egg yolk, garlic, and ground nutmeg.

Season with salt and pepper to taste and set aside.

Assembling the ravioli:

Place the dough between two pieces of parchment paper, and roll out the pasta to its thinnest point possible. Slice into 2-inch strips and then cut into evenly sized squares about 2x2-inches.

Heap roughly a tablespoon of filling onto the dough. Drape a second piece over it, and press down around the edges to seal, removing any air bubbles.

Trim the edges close to the filling using a cookie cutter knife or pizza cutter.

Place all the ravioli on a baking tray, and freeze for 15 minutes to firm them up.

For cooking:

In a large skillet, add 1 tablespoon of olive oil and heat on low.

Add ravioli and cook until golden on both sides.

Toss with your favorite sauce and serve.

For the spinach filling:

1 tablespoon avocado oil for cooking

2 cloves garlic, minced

14 ounces spinach

1 cup ricotta cheese

¼ cup Parmesan cheese, freshly grated

¼ cup pine nuts, lightly toasted

¼ teaspoon ground nutmeg

1 egg yolk

Salt and ground black pepper, to taste

Calories per serving 86
Total fat 5g
Total carbohydrates 6g
Fiber 3g; *Net carbs 3g*
Protein 4g

SOFT PRETZELS

PREP TIME 15 MINUTES | COOK TIME 15 MINUTES | MAKES 6 PRETZELS

2 cups blanched almond flour

1 tablespoon baking powder

1 teaspoon garlic powder

1 teaspoon onion powder

3 large eggs, divided

3 cups low-moisture mozzarella cheese, shredded

5 tablespoons cream cheese

Coarse sea salt, for topping

Calories per serving 453
Total fat 37g
Total carbohydrates 11g
Fiber 4g; *Net carbs 7g*
Protein 28g

Directions

Preheat oven to 425°F. Line a baking sheet with parchment paper.

In a medium mixing bowl, combine the almond flour, baking powder, garlic powder, and onion powder. Mix until thoroughly combined.

Crack one egg into a small bowl, and whisk to make the egg wash.

In a saucepan over low heat, combine the shredded mozzarella and cream cheese. Stir continuously until completely melted.

Add the remaining 2 eggs and the almond flour mixture. Mix until well combined. Add the cheese mixture, and continue mixing until a dough forms.

Using your hands, divide the dough into 6 equal portions. Roll each portion into a long rope. Spray the dough as you roll to make the dough easier to handle and ensure it stays moist.

Fold each piece into the shape of a pretzel, and brush the top, with the egg wash.

Sprinkle sea salt on top and bake on the middle rack for 12 to 14 minutes or until golden brown.

Serve warm.

SOURDOUGH BAGUETTES

PREP TIME 15 MINUTES | COOK TIME 40-55 MINUTES | MAKES 8 BAGUETTES

1 ½ cups almond flour

⅓ cup psyllium husk powder

½ cup coconut flour

½ cup flax meal, packed

1 teaspoon baking soda

1 teaspoon sea salt

6 large egg whites

2 large eggs

¾ cup almond milk

¼ cup apple cider vinegar

1 cup lukewarm water

½ tablespoon lemon juice

Calories per serving 254
Total fat 13g
Total carbohydrates 8g
Fiber 16g; *Net carbs 8g*
Protein 10g

Directions

Preheat the oven to 360°F. Line a baking sheet with parchment paper.

In a large bowl, combine all of the dry ingredients.

In a separate bowl, mix the eggs, egg whites, and almond milk.

Using an electric mixer, combine the dry ingredients with the egg mixture.

Add vinegar, lukewarm water, and lemon juice. Continue mixing until well combined (do not over-process the dough).

Using a spoon, form 8 baguettes on the baking sheet (these will rise, so make sure to leave some space between them).

Score the tops of the baguettes diagonally, and make 3 to 4 cuts.

Bake for 10 minutes, then reduce the temperature to 300°F and bake for an additional 30 to 45 minutes.

Remove from the oven, and place the baguettes on a rack to cool completely.

Once cooled, slice and serve.

SPINACH FETA BREAD

PREP TIME 2 MINUTES | COOK TIME 15 MINUTES | SERVES 1

1 large egg

1 tablespoon coconut flour

1 tablespoon almond flour

1 tablespoon butter, melted

1 tablespoon almond milk

¼ teaspoon baking powder

½ teaspoon garlic powder

⅛ teaspoon salt

¼ cup spinach, finely chopped

1 tablespoon feta cheese, crumbled

Directions

Preheat oven to 400°F. Grease a ramekin with butter.

In a small bowl, beat the egg, and add the coconut flour, almond flour, baking powder, salt, almond milk, and butter. Stir to combine.

Add the spinach, garlic powder, and feta, and stir until evenly distributed.

Spoon the mixture into the ramekin, and bake for 10 to 15 minutes.

Allow them to cool for 5 minutes, then invert the ramekin, and take the bread out.

Calories per serving 253
Total fat 21g
Total carbohydrates 8g
Fiber 4g; *Net carbs 4g*
Protein 9g

HERBED LINGUINE

PREP TIME 10 MINUTES | COOK TIME 10 MINUTES | SERVES 1

½ cup cream cheese

3 extra-large eggs

¼ teaspoon sea salt

¼ teaspoon dried oregano

½ teaspoon dried basil

¼ teaspoon garlic powder

3 teaspoons almond flour

½ teaspoon xanthan gum

Calories per serving 244
Total fat 20g
Total carbohydrates 2g
Fiber 0g; **Net carbs 2g**
Protein 14g

Directions

Whisk cream cheese and 1 egg until well combined. Whisk in xanthan gum, and continue whisking until smooth, then incorporate the remaining eggs, one at a time, and finally add salt, oregano, basil, garlic powder, and almond flour.

Pre-heat oven to 320°F. Line two baking sheets with parchment paper.

Pour the egg mixture over baking sheets, and spread as thinly and as evenly as you can, in a square or rectangular pattern.

Bake for 10-12 minutes, until opaque over the top and the edges have shrunk in.

Remove from oven and allow to cool slightly.

Begin to peel away from the baking sheet and flip over.

Once cooled, slice very thin with a sharp knife.

Transfer to a plate or tray.

Allow linguine to air-dry for a few hours before adding to your sauce.

FETTUCCINE

PREP TIME 2 MINUTES | COOK TIME 8 MINUTES | SERVES 1

2 eggs

1 ounce cream cheese

¼ teaspoon garlic powder

Pinch of salt

Calories per serving 244
Total fat 20g
Total carbohydrates 2g
Fiber 0g; *Net carbs 2g*
Protein 14g

Directions

Preheat oven to 325°F, and grease an 8x8-inch baking dish.

In a blender, combine all of the ingredients. Blend until smooth.

Pour mixture into baking dish, and bake for 8 minutes or until just set.

Remove from the oven, and allow to cool for about 5 minutes.

With a spatula, gently remove the sheet of "pasta" from the pan, and place on a large cutting board. Slice lengthwise with a pizza cutter into ⅛-inch thick slices. If you don't have a pizza cutter, a sharp knife will work as well.

Mix with your favorite sauce and serve.

ALMOND FLOUR FETTUCCINE

PREP TIME 30 MINUTES | COOK TIME 1 MINUTES | SERVES 4

½ cup cream cheese

3 extra large eggs

¼ teaspoon sea salt

3 teaspoons almond flour

½ teaspoon xanthan gum

Calories per serving 656
Total fat 57g
Total carbohydrates 8g
Fiber 2g; *Net carbs 6g*
Protein 27g

Directions

Whisk cream cheese and 1 egg until well combined. Whisk in xanthan gum, and continue whisking until smooth, then incorporate the remaining eggs, 1 at a time, and finally add salt and almond flour.

Pre-heat oven to 320°F. Line two baking sheets with parchment paper

Pour the egg mixture over baking sheets, and spread as thinly and as evenly as you can, in a square or rectangular pattern.

Bake for 10-12 minutes, until opaque over the top and the edges have shrunk in.

Remove from oven and allow to cool slightly.

Begin to peel away from the baking sheet and flip over.

Once cooled, slice into thin strips with a pizza cutter or sharp knife.

Transfer to a plate or tray.

Allow the fettuccine to air-dry for a few hours before adding to your sauce.

CHEESY GARLIC BREAD

½ cup mozzarella cheese, shredded

¼ cup almond meal or flour

1 egg, whisked

2 tablespoons cream cheese

2 tablespoons butter, melted

1 tablespoon garlic, crushed

1 tablespoon parsley, fresh or dried

1 teaspoon baking powder

Salt, to taste

Calories per serving 141
Total fat 13g
Total carbohydrates 2g
Fiber 0g; **Net carbs 2g**
Protein 5g

Directions

Preheat oven to 425°F. Line a baking sheet with parchment paper.

In a saucepan over medium heat, combine all ingredients except the egg, butter, parsley, and garlic. Stir until cheese is completely melted and all ingredients are well combined.

Remove from heat, and slowly add the egg. Mix until completely incorporated, and a dough has formed.

Place dough on a baking tray, and form into a garlic bread shape.

In a small bowl, combine butter, parsley, and garlic. Brush over the top of the dough, and sprinkle with more cheese if desired.

Bake for 15 minutes or until golden brown.

CAULIFLOWER BREAD BUNS

PREP TIME 20 MINUTES | COOK TIME 25 MINUTES | MAKES 5 BUNS

3 cups finely riced cauliflower

2 large eggs

½ cup Parmesan cheese, shredded

2 tablespoons almond flour

2 tablespoons coconut flour

½ teaspoon baking powder

½ teaspoon Italian seasonings

Pinch of salt

Calories per serving 386
Total fat 26g
Total carbohydrates 6g
Fiber 1g; *Net carbs 5g*
Protein 31g

Directions

Preheat oven to 400°F. Line a baking sheet with parchment paper.

In a large bowl, combine cauliflower, eggs, cheese, almond flour, coconut flour, baking powder, Italian seasoning, and salt. Mix with a large spoon until thoroughly combined.

Lightly pack the cauliflower mixture, and measure out ½ cup. Dump each ½ cup onto a baking sheet, and press down with your palm to compact the mixture. Form bread into 4-inch circles.

Bake for 20 to 25 minutes or until tops are golden brown.

Allow to cool slightly before using.

CHEESY ROSEMARY FOCACCIA BREAD

PREP TIME 10 MINUTES | COOK TIME 55 MINUTES | SERVES 8-10

1 medium head of cauliflower, riced

½ cup Parmesan cheese

¾ cup thick plain yogurt

2 eggs

1 cup cheddar cheese, shredded, divided

1 teaspoon garlic powder

1 tablespoon fresh rosemary, finely chopped

Salt and ground black pepper, to taste

Calories per serving 224
Total fat 14g
Total carbohydrates 7g
Fiber 2g; *Net carbs 5g*
Protein 17g

Directions

Preheat oven to 400°F. Lightly grease a 9-inch pie dish

Using a food processor, pulse cauliflower florets until riced.

In a large bowl, combine riced cauliflower along with ½ of the cheddar cheese and remaining ingredients, and mix until thoroughly combined.

Pour mixture into pie dish, and press down evenly.

Bake for 45 minutes or until all of the water is cooked out of the cauliflower.

Remove from oven, and sprinkle remaining ½ cup of cheddar cheese over the top. Return to the oven, and cook for an additional 10 minutes.

Cut into slices, serve.

ITALIAN CLOUD BREAD

4 large eggs, separated

½ teaspoon cream of tartar

2 ounces cream cheese

½ teaspoon dried basil

½ teaspoon dried oregano

½ teaspoon sea salt

½ teaspoon garlic powder

Calories per serving 50
Total fat 4g
Total carbohydrates 1g
Fiber 0g; **Net carbs 1g**
Protein 3g

Directions

Preheat the oven to 300°F. Line two baking sheets with parchment paper.

Separate the egg whites and egg yolks. Using an electric mixer, begin to beat egg whites.

Add the cream of tartar, and beat until stiff peaks form.

In a separate bowl, beat the cream cheese until softened. Add the egg yolks one at a time, and mix until completely smooth. Add in the basil, oregano, salt, and garlic powder.

Gently fold the firm meringue into the yolk mixture, making sure not to deflate the egg whites as much as possible.

Spoon ¼-cup portions of the foam onto the baking sheets, and spread into even 4-inch circles. Make sure to leave space around each circle.

Bake for up to 30 minutes or until golden brown and the center does not jiggle when shaken.

Cool for several minutes on the baking sheets.

CROISSANTS

3 cups mozzarella cheese, shredded

2 ounces cream cheese

3 egg whites

½ cup coconut flour

2 tablespoons unsalted butter, melted

1 tablespoon psyllium husk powder

¼ teaspoon cream of tartar

2 tablespoons, plain sparkling water, room temperature

¼ teaspoon salt

Calories per serving 117
Total fat 8g
Total carbohydrates 3g
Fiber 2g; *Net carbs 1g*
Protein 6g

Directions

Preheat the oven to 385°F. Line a baking sheet with parchment paper.

In a saucepan over low heat, melt the mozzarella and cream cheese together. Stir until smooth and creamy.

Using an electric mixer, beat egg whites and cream of tartar until stiff peaks form.

Slowly fold in coconut flour, psyllium husk, and salt.

Knead with your hands until you achieve a dough-like consistency.

Add sparkling water and continue kneading.

Place the dough between two sheets of parchment paper, and roll the dough to ⅓-inch thickness.

Brush half of the melted butter onto the dough.

With a pizza cutter, start by dividing the dough into 4 equal squares, then into triangles that are about 4 inches wide at the bottom.

Roll the triangles up starting at the wide part and finishing with the point.

Place each croissant on the baking sheet at least 2 inches apart.

Brush the tops of the croissants with remaining butter, and bake them for 12 minutes or until golden brown.

Allow to cool slightly before serving.

COCONUT FLOUR BREAD

PREP TIME 15 MINUTES | COOK TIME 35 MINUTES | MAKES 14 SLICES

6 eggs

⅓ cup coconut oil

⅓ cup almond milk

½ cup coconut flour

½ cup ground flaxseed

2 tablespoons monk fruit sweetener

1 tablespoon baking powder

1 teaspoon arrowroot powder

½ teaspoon salt

½ teaspoon ground cinnamon

Calories per serving 117
Total fat 10g
Total carbohydrates 4g
Fiber 3g; *Net carbs 1g*
Protein 4g

Directions

Preheat oven to 375°F. Line a 8x4-inch loaf pan with parchment paper.

Using an electric mixer, combine eggs, coconut oil, and almond milk. Mix until well combined.

Add the remaining ingredients, and mix until thoroughly incorporated.

Pour batter in loaf pan, and tap the bottom a few times to remove any bubbles.

Bake for 40 to 45 minutes or until a toothpick in center comes out clean.

Cool for at least 20 minutes before transferring to a wire rack.

Cool completely before slicing.

ENGLISH MUFFINS

PREP TIME 5 MINUTES | COOK TIME 3-4 MINUTES | MAKES 6 MUFFINS

2 eggs

2 tablespoons coconut flour

½ teaspoon baking powder

Salt, to taste

Butter, for cooking

Calories per serving 169
Total fat 17g
Total carbohydrates 1g
Fiber 1g; *Net carbs 0g*
Protein 3g

Directions

Preheat oven to 400°F, and grease 6 wells of a large muffin tin.

In a large bowl, combine coconut flour, baking powder, and salt.

Add the eggs, and whisk until thoroughly mixed. Allow the batter to sit for 5 minutes.

Scoop batter evenly into the bottom of the muffin well, and smooth with a spoon.

Bake for 10 minutes.

Allow to cool completely before removing.

EVERYTHING BAGELS

PREP TIME 15 MINUTES | COOK TIME 10-14 MINUTES | MAKES 6 BAGELS

1 ½ cups almond flour

1 tablespoon baking powder

2 ½ cups mozzarella cheese, shredded

2 ounces cream cheese, cubed

1 tablespoon butter, melted (for brushing bagels with)

2 large eggs

Poppy seeds

Dried minced onion

Sea salt

Calories per serving 397
Total fat 33g
Total carbohydrates 6g
Fiber 4g; *Net carbs 2g*
Protein 21g

Directions

Preheat the oven to 400°F. Line a baking sheet with parchment paper.

In a bowl, combine the almond flour and baking powder. Set aside.

In a saucepan over low heat, melt the shredded mozzarella and cubed cream cheese. Stir frequently.

Stir the melted cheese mixture, into the flour mixture and add the eggs one at a time.

Knead with your hands until a dough forms (the dough will be very sticky).

Divide the dough into 6 parts. Roll a long log with each part, and join the ends to make a bagel shape. Repeat with the remaining dough.

Brush top of bagels with melted butter, and sprinkle with poppy seeds, dried onion, and sea salt.

Bake for 10 to 14 minutes until the bagels are firm and golden.

Allow bagels to cool before serving.

FATHEAD PIZZA CRUST

1 ½ cups mozzarella cheese, shredded

2 tablespoons cream cheese, cubed

2 large eggs (beaten)

⅓ cup coconut flour

Calories per serving 266
Total fat 18g
Total carbohydrates 7g
Fiber 3g; *Net carbs 4g*
Protein 18g

Directions

Preheat the oven to 425°F. Line a baking sheet or pizza pan with parchment paper.

In a saucepan over low heat, combine the shredded mozzarella and cubed cream cheese. Stir continuously until completely melted.

Add the eggs and coconut flour, and stir until combined.

Transfer mixture into a large bowl, and knead with your hands until a dough forms.

Place dough onto the baking pan and flatten with your hands or a rolling pin to ¼-inch or ⅓-inch thick (if using a rolling pin, place dough between two pieces of parchment paper to prevent sticking).

Use a toothpick or fork to poke holes throughout the crust to prevent bubbling.

Bake for 6 minutes. Poke more holes in any places where you see bubbles forming. Bake for an additional 3 to 7 minutes, or until golden brown.

FLAX TORTILLAS

PREP TIME 1 HOUR 20 MINUTES | COOK TIME 3 MINUTES | MAKES 10 TORTILLAS

1 cup almond flour

¾ cup flaxmeal, packed

¼ cup coconut flour

2 tablespoons psyllium husks, whole

2 tablespoons chia seeds, ground

1 teaspoon salt

1 cup water, lukewarm, + 2-4 tablespoons (if the dough is too dry)

2 tablespoons butter, for greasing the pan

Calories per serving 121
Total fat 9g
Total carbohydrates 8g
Fiber 8g; **Net carbs 0g**
Protein 3g

Directions

In a large bowl combine flaxmeal, coconut flour, almond flour, salt, and psyllium husks.

Add the ground chia seeds, and stir until well-incorporated.

Slowly add the water, and mix with your hands until dough begins to form (if needed, add a few more tablespoons of water).

Allow the dough to rest in the refrigerator for up to one hour.

Remove from the fridge, and cut the dough into 6 equal pieces.

Place a piece of the dough between two pieces of parchment paper and roll out until the dough is very thin.

Use an 8-inch lid or bowl to cut out the tortillas. Repeat with the remaining dough and the cut-offs until you get 10 tortillas.

Grease a large pan with butter, and place over medium heat. One at a time, place the tortillas in the pan and cook for 1 to 2 minutes on each side until lightly browned.

FRENCH BRIOCHE

6 egg whites and 3 egg yolks, separated

½ cup salted butter

1 cup superfine almond flour

¼ teaspoon cream of tartar

1 ½ teaspoons baking powder

Calories per serving 246
Total fat 18g
Total carbohydrates 8g
Fiber 1g; *Net carbs 7g*
Protein 6g

Directions

Preheat the oven at 350°F, and lightly grease 6 wells of a large muffin tin.

In a saucepan over low heat, melt the butter slowly.

Using an electric mixer, beat the egg whites and cream of tartar until soft peaks form.

In a separate bowl, combine the egg yolks, butter, baking powder, and almond flour. Mix well.

Gently fold the flour mixture into the egg whites until thoroughly combined.

Pour the batter into 6 muffin wells, and bake for about 20 to 30 minutes or until golden brown.

Cool completely on cooling rack before serving. Store in the fridge for up to 5 days.

HERBED CAVATELLI

PREP TIME 40 MINUTES | COOK TIME 5 MINUTES | SERVES 4

¾ cup almond flour

2 tablespoons coconut flour

2 teaspoons arrowroot powder

¼ teaspoon kosher salt

½ teaspoon dried Italian seasoning

2 teaspoons apple cider vinegar

1 egg, lightly beaten

2-4 teaspoons water, as needed

Calories per serving 77
Total fat 4g
Total carbohydrates 7g
Fiber 2g; **Net carbs 5g**
Protein 3g

Directions

In a food processor, combine almond flour, coconut flour, arrowroot powder, Italian seasoning, and salt. Pulse until thoroughly combined.

With the food processor running, add in apple cider vinegar. Once it has distributed evenly, add in the egg.

Add water teaspoon by teaspoon, as needed, until the dough forms into a ball. The dough should be firm, but sticky to touch and with no creases.

Wrap dough in plastic wrap and knead it through the plastic for a couple minutes.

Place the dough in the refrigerator to rest for 30 minutes (or up to 5 days).

Cut dough into 4 pieces, roll out into logs, and slice off even sized pieces. This will create evenly sized pasta. Lightly dust a cutting board and pasta pieces with coconut flour. Place a piece of pasta on your cutting board, and use a knife to press the dough upwards and towards you. This will curl the pasta into the shape you want.

Place shaped pasta in the freezer for 15 minutes.

In a skillet over low heat, add butter and oil. Once warm, add in chilled pasta and toss.

For *al dente* pasta, cook until it just begins to develop some color.

Toss pasta with your favorite sauce.

PAN FRIED GNOCCHI

PREP TIME 30 MINUTES | COOK TIME 8 MINUTES | SERVES 2

2 cups low moisture mozzarella, shredded

3 egg yolks

1 teaspoon salt

¼ teaspoon ground nutmeg

Butter, for cooking

Calories per serving 809
Total fat 53g
Total carbohydrates 1g
Fiber 0g; *Net carbs 1g*
Protein 5g

Directions

In a saucepan over low heat, add mozzarella. Stir continuously until completely melted.

Separate 3 egg yolks and beat them to combine.

Pour half the egg yolks at a time into the melted mozzarella, along with the ground nutmeg, and stir to combine.

Transfer the dough onto a piece of parchment paper.

Divide the dough into fourths, and roll each piece into a long, thin strip.

Cut dough into 1-inch pieces. Press gently with a fork to make them look like traditional gnocchi.

Bring a large pot of water to a boil, and drop the gnocchi in. Boil them for about 1 minute or until they all float to the top.

Drain completely.

Heat a large skillet over medium to high heat, and melt a small pat of butter.

Fry gnocchi on both sides until golden brown on each side.

Top with your favorite toppings.

FATHEAD BUNS

PREP TIME 10 MINUTES | COOK TIME 15 MINUTES | MAKES 4 BUNS

2 ounces cream cheese

¾ cup mozzarella cheese, shredded

½ cup cheddar cheese, shredded

1 egg, beaten

⅓ cup almond flour

¼ teaspoon onion powder

2 teaspoons baking powder

Calories per serving 211
Total fat 18g
Total carbohydrates 2g
Fiber 0g; **Net carbs 2g**
Protein 12g

Directions

Preheat the oven to 425°F. Line a baking sheet with parchment paper.

In a saucepan over low heat, combine the cream cheese and mozzarella. Stir continuously until completely melted.

In a separate bowl, whisk egg until beaten. Add the dry ingredients, and continue mixing until well combined.

Add mozzarella mixture and the shredded cheddar cheese to the dough (the dough will be sticky).

Spoon dough onto a piece of plastic wrap. Lightly dust the top of it with almond flour.

Fold the plastic wrap over the dough and gently start working into a ball.

Place dough ball in the refrigerator for 30 minutes.

Cut the dough into 4 equal portions, and roll each portion into a ball. Cut the ball in half (this is your top and bottom bun).

Place cut side down on parchment paper, and bake for 10 to 12 minutes or until golden brown.

Store in the refrigerator for up to 5 days until ready to use.